INTERMEDIATE SET #2

RUDIMENTS EXAM SERIES ANSWERS

By Glory St. Germain ARCT RMT MYCC UMTC &
Shelagh McKibbon-U'Ren RMT UMTC

GSG MUSIC

Enriching Lives Through Music Education

ISBN: 978-1-927641-13-2

The Ultimate Music Theory™ Program
Enriching Lives Through Music Education

The Ultimate Music Theory™ Workbooks & Answer Books Program includes:

UMT Rudiments Workbooks for Prep 1, Prep 2, Basic, Intermediate, Advanced & Complete
UMT Exam Series (Set #1 & Set #2) for Preparatory, Basic, Intermediate & Advanced

Supplemental Workbooks for PREP LEVEL, LEVELS 1 - 8 & COMPLETE LEVEL
UMT Supplemental Exam Series for LEVEL 5, LEVEL 6, LEVEL 7 & LEVEL 8

The Ultimate Music Theory Program is the *Way to Score Success* as UMT helps students prepare for nationally recognized theory examinations including the Royal Conservatory of Music.

Library and Archives Canada Cataloguing in Publication. UMT Workbooks & Exam Series /Glory St. Germain & Shelagh McKibbon-U'Ren. Respect Copyright. All rights reserved. GlorylandPublishing.com

Ultimate Music Theory Rudiments Exam Series

GP - EPS1	ISBN: 978-1-927641-00-2	Preparatory Rudiments Exams Set #1
GP - EPS1A	ISBN: 978-1-927641-08-8	Preparatory Exams Answers Set #1
GP - EPS2	ISBN: 978-1-927641-01-9	Preparatory Rudiments Exams Set #2
GP - EPS2A	ISBN: 978-1-927641-09-5	Preparatory Exams Answers Set #2
GP - EBS1	ISBN: 978-1-927641-02-6	Basic Rudiments Exams Set #1
GP - EBS1A	ISBN: 978-1-927641-10-1	Basic Exams Answers Set #1
GP - EBS2	ISBN: 978-1-927641-03-3	Basic Rudiments Exams Set #2
GP - EBS2A	ISBN: 978-1-927641-11-8	Basic Exams Answers Set #2
GP - EIS1	ISBN: 978-1-927641-04-0	Intermediate Rudiments Exams Set #1
GP - EIS1A	ISBN: 978-1-927641-12-5	Intermediate Exams Answers Set #1
GP - EIS2	ISBN: 978-1-927641-05-7	Intermediate Rudiments Exams Set #2
GP - EIS2A	ISBN: 978-1-927641-13-2	Intermediate Exams Answers Set #2
GP - EAS1	ISBN: 978-1-927641-06-4	Advanced Rudiments Exams Set #1
GP - EAS1A	ISBN: 978-1-927641-14-9	Advanced Exams Answers Set #1
GP - EAS2	ISBN: 978-1-927641-07-1	Advanced Rudiments Exams Set #2
GP - EAS2A	ISBN: 978-1-927641-15-6	Advanced Exams Answers Set #2

Ultimate Music Theory Supplemental Exam Series

GP-L5E	ISBN: 978-1-990358-11-1	LEVEL 5 Exams
GP-L5EA	ISBN: 978-1-990358-12-8	LEVEL 5 Exams Answers
GP-L6E	ISBN: 978-1-990358-13-5	LEVEL 6 Exams
GP-L6EA	ISBN: 978-1-990358-14-2	LEVEL 6 Exams Answers
GP-L7E	ISBN: 978-1-990358-15-9	LEVEL 7 Exams
GP-L7EA	ISBN: 978-1-990358-16-6	LEVEL 7 Exams Answers
GP-L8E	ISBN: 978-1-990358-17-3	LEVEL 8 Exams
GP-L8EA	ISBN: 978-1-990358-18-0	LEVEL 8 Exams Answers

Go to UltimateMusicTheory.com and check out the FREE Resources

Ultimate Music Theory FREE RESOURCES created just for you!

The **Ultimate Music Theory Exams** reinforce the **UMT Intermediate Rudiments Workbook** and prepare students for continued learning with UMT Advanced Rudiments.

Intermediate Rudiments Theory Examination requirements include Basic Rudiments requirements plus the following:

Pitch
- Double sharps and double flats

Rhythm
- Note and rest time values (breve, whole, half, quarter, eighth, sixteenth and thirty-second)
- Double dotted notes
- Time Signatures in Simple Time and in Compound Time
- Irregular groups in Simple Time (quintuplets and septuplets)

Scales in Major and minor keys up to and including seven sharps and seven flats
- Write or identify: Major and minor (natural, harmonic and melodic) scales, ascending and descending
- Write or identify: Related keys: relative Major and minor, tonic (parallel) Major and minor; enharmonic Major and minor
- Write or identify: Technical degree names of the scale degrees
- Write or identify: Whole-tone scales and chromatic scales (using any standard version)
- Identify: blues scales, Major pentatonic scales, minor pentatonic scales and octatonic scales

Triads in all Major and harmonic minor keys
- Write: Solid (blocked) in Root Position and inversions (close position only)
- Identify: Solid (blocked) or broken in Root Position and inversions (close position or open position)

Intervals - Perfect, Major and minor
- Write or identify: above or below a given note, all intervals and their inversions up to and including an octave, melodic or harmonic form (with or without a Key Signature)

Recognition of Key Signatures up to and including seven sharps and seven flats
- Identify the key (Major or minor) of a given melody with a Key Signature
- Rewrite the excerpt using the correct Key Signature and identify the key (Major or minor)

Transposition (Major Keys up to and including seven sharps and seven flats)
- Transpose a melody up or down any interval within the octave

Cadences in all Major and harmonic minor keys
- Identify cadences in keyboard style only in a musical excerpt
- Perfect (Authentic): V - I (Major) and V - i (minor); Plagal: IV - I (Major) and iv - i (minor); Imperfect (Half Cadence): I - V or IV - V (Major) and i - V or iv - V (minor)

Musical Terms and Signs
- Recognize, define or supply the musical terms or signs as listed in the Intermediate Rudiments Workbook

Analysis
- Analyze a short musical composition, identifying any of the above theory requirements

Score:
   60 - 69 Pass; 70 - 79 Honors; 80 - 89 First Class Honors; 90 - 100 First Class Honors with Distinction

Ultimate Music Theory: *The Way to Score Success!*

UltimateMusicTheory.com © Copyright 2013 Gloryland Publishing. All Rights Reserved.

ULTIMATE MUSIC THEORY
INTERMEDIATE EXAM SET #2 - EXAM #1

Total Score: ____ / 100

> ♪ **UMT Tip:** Before beginning your exam, write out the Circle of Fifths. Write the order of flats and sharps. Write the Major keys on the outside of the circle and the relative minor keys on the inside of the circle.

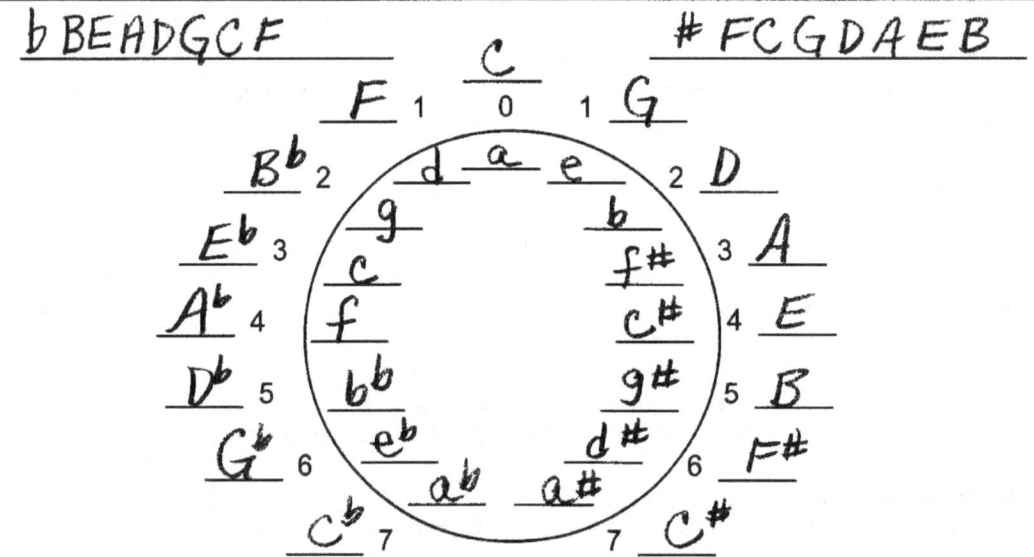

> ♪ **UMT Tip:** When writing an interval of a harmonic Aug 1, and both notes require accidentals, write the touching notes first. Then add BOTH accidentals in front of the touching notes. The lower accidental is always written first. (♭♮ or ♮♯ etc.)

1. a) Name the following harmonic intervals.

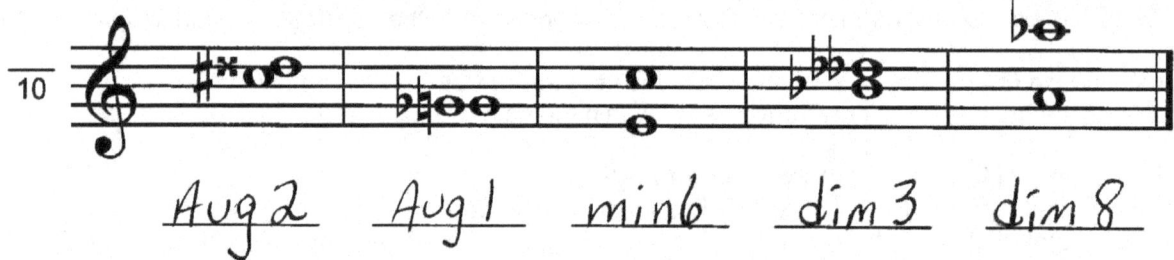

Aug 2   Aug 1   min 6   dim 3   dim 8

b) Invert the above harmonic intervals in the given clef. Name the inversions.

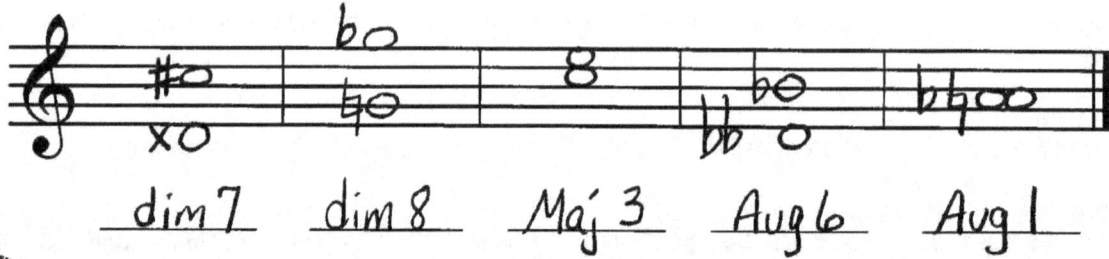

dim 7   dim 8   Maj 3   Aug 6   Aug 1

UltimateMusicTheory.com © Copyright 2013 Gloryland Publishing. All Rights Reserved.

ULTIMATE MUSIC THEORY
INTERMEDIATE EXAM SET #2 - EXAM #1

> ♪ **UMT Tip:** A triad in close position is written as close together as possible. No interval is larger than a 6th.

2. a) Write the following solid triads in close position in the Treble Clef. Use the correct Key Signature and any necessary accidentals. Use whole notes.

Tonic triad of	Submediant triad of	Dominant triad of
b minor harmonic	B Major	D flat Major
in second inversion	in root position	in first inversion

b) Write the following solid triads in close position in the Bass Clef. Use accidentals. Use whole notes.

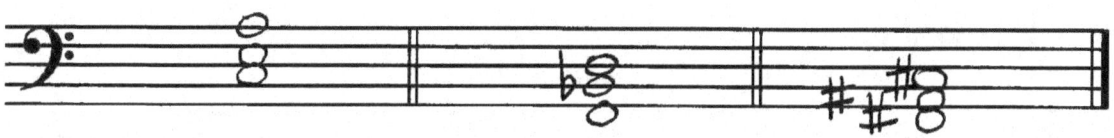

Mediant triad of	Submediant triad of	Subdominant triad of
F Major	d minor harmonic	C sharp Major
in first inversion	in second inversion	in root position

> ♪ **UMT Tip:** A triad in open position is written with intervals that can be larger than a 6th. One of the notes (usually the Root) may be doubled.

c) Identify the root note and the quality/type of each of the following open position triads.

Root Note: __G__ __Db__ __G#__ __Ab__

Quality/Type: __Major__ __minor__ __Major__ __minor__

ULTIMATE MUSIC THEORY
INTERMEDIATE EXAM SET #2 - EXAM #1

> ♪ **UMT Tip:** Rewrite the bar lines first before transposing the notes.

3. The following melody is in the key of B Major.
   a) Transpose the given melody UP a diminished fifth. Use the correct Key Signature.
   b) Name the key of the new melody.

Key: B Major

Key: __F Major__

> ♪ **UMT Tip:** Name the accidentals in order of the Key Signature. A melodic fragment may not contain all the accidentals in the key.

The following melody has been written using accidentals instead of a Key Signature.
c) Name the key of the given melody.
d) Rewrite the given melody using the correct Key Signature and any necessary accidentals.

Key: __Ab Major__   Flats: __Bb Eb Ab Db__

ULTIMATE MUSIC THEORY
INTERMEDIATE EXAM SET #2 - EXAM #1

> ♪ **UMT Tip:** Count the number of notes and identify the pattern of tones and semitones.

4. Name the following scales as Major, natural minor, harmonic minor, melodic minor, blues, Major pentatonic, minor pentatonic, octatonic, chromatic or whole tone.

a) natural minor

b) blues

c) harmonic minor

d) chromatic

e) whole tone

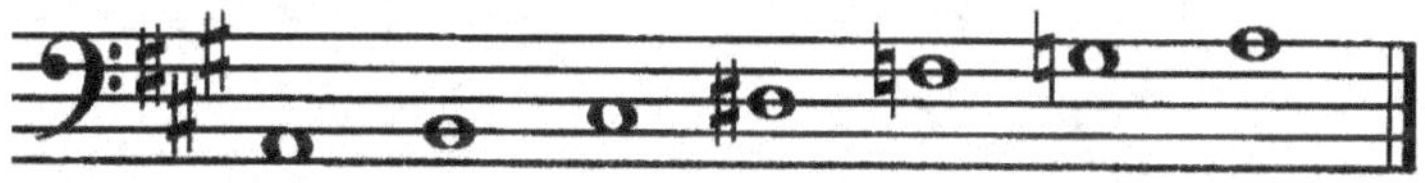

f) Major

g) Major pentatonic

h) octatonic

i) minor pentatonic

j) melodic minor

ULTIMATE MUSIC THEORY
INTERMEDIATE EXAM SET #2 - EXAM #1

> ♪ **UMT Tip:** A Perfect Cadence and a Plagal Cadence both end on the Tonic. An Imperfect Cadence ends on the Dominant. Identify the key by identifying if the final bass note is the Tonic or Dominant in the Major key or in the relative minor key.

5. For each of the following cadences, name:
   a) the key.
   b) the type of cadence (Perfect, Plagal or Imperfect).

Key: G Major   c minor   B Major
Type: Perfect   Imperfect   Imperfect

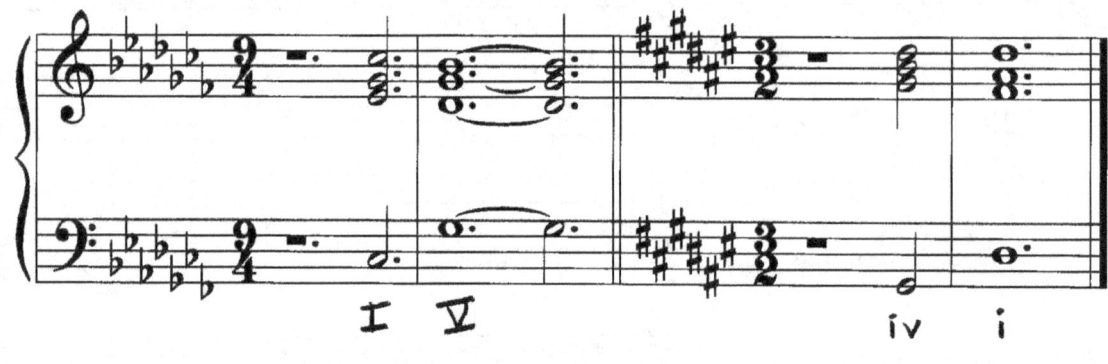

Key: Cb Major   d# minor
Type: Imperfect   Plagal

UltimateMusicTheory.com © Copyright 2013 Gloryland Publishing. All Rights Reserved.

ULTIMATE MUSIC THEORY
INTERMEDIATE EXAM SET #2 - EXAM #1

> ♪ **UMT Tip:** Melodic fragments do not always start or end on the Tonic note. Look for accidentals which may indicate the raised 7th of a minor key.

6. For each of the following excerpts:
   a) Name the key.
   b) Add the correct Time Signature below the bracket.

___
10

Key: b minor

Key: C# Major

Key: d minor

Key: A♭ Major

Key: a♭ minor

ULTIMATE MUSIC THEORY
INTERMEDIATE EXAM SET #2 - EXAM #1

> ♪ **UMT Tip:** Irregular groups are played in the time of a regular group of the same note value.
> In Simple Time, 3 = 2, and 5, 6 or 7 = 4.
> In Compound Time, 2 = 3, 4 = 3 and 5 or 7 = 3 or 6.

7. Add rests below each bracket to complete each measure.

ULTIMATE MUSIC THEORY
INTERMEDIATE EXAM SET #2 - EXAM #1

♪ **UMT Tip:** Use the Circle of Fifths to identify the Key Signature.

8. a) Name the following notes.

    ___
    10

    The Submediant of C Major is ____A____.

    The Tonic of F sharp Major is ____F#____.

    The Subdominant of c sharp minor harmonic is ____F#____.

    The Leading note of f minor harmonic is ____E____.

    The Supertonic of c minor is ____D____.

    b) For each of the following, name the Major key. Identify the technical degree name of the note.

    Major key: ____Eb Major____   ____E Major____   ____D Major____
    Technical degree name: ____Mediant____   ____Subdominant____   ____Leading note____

    Major key: ____B Major____   ____Gb Major____
    Technical degree name: ____Supertonic____   ____Submediant____

UltimateMusicTheory.com © Copyright 2013 Gloryland Publishing. All Rights Reserved.

ULTIMATE MUSIC THEORY
INTERMEDIATE EXAM SET #2 - EXAM #1

> ♪ **UMT Tip:** Read the instructions carefully. Identify each Term and then match it to the correct definition.

9. Match each English definition with its Italian term. (Not all terms will be used.)

Definition		Term	
Maelzel's metronome	c	a)	e
brilliant	g	b)	alla
almost, as if	h	c)	M.M.
with movement	i	d)	non
and	a	e)	poco a poco
more	j	f)	rubato
not	d	g)	brillante
in the manner of	b	h)	quasi
little by little	e	i)	con moto
with some freedom of tempo to enhance musical expression	f	j)	più
		k)	animato

ULTIMATE MUSIC THEORY
INTERMEDIATE EXAM SET #2 - EXAM #1

> ♪ **UMT Tip:** The Time Signature is written in both the Treble Clef and the Bass Clef.

10. Analyze the following excerpt by answering the questions below.

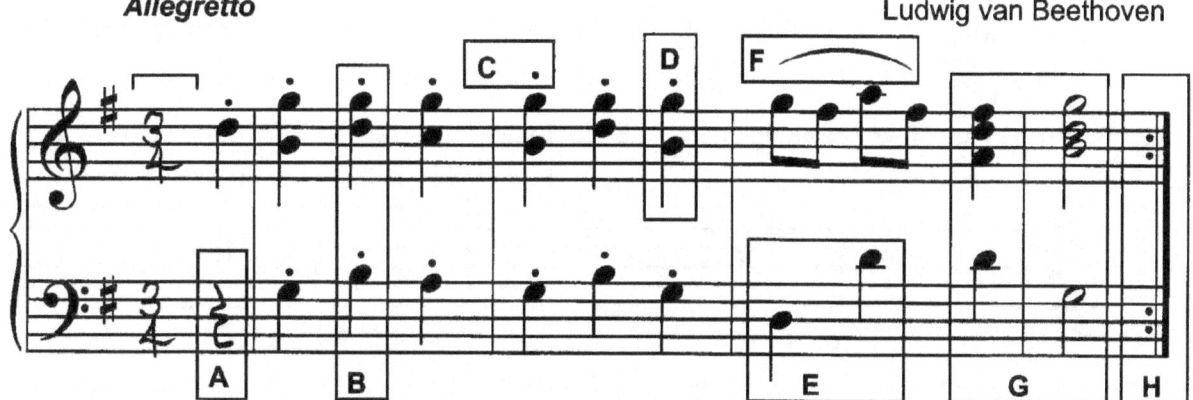

a) Name the key of this piece. __G Major__

b) Explain the tempo of this piece. __Allegretto - fairly fast (a little slower than allegro)__

c) Add the Time Signature directly on the music.

d) Add the missing rest at the letter **A**.

e) For the triad at **B**, name: Root: __G__ Type/Quality: __Major__ Position: __1st inv.__

f) Explain the sign at the letter **C**. __staccato - detached__

g) Name the intervals at the following letters: D __min 6__ E __Per 8__

h) Explain the sign at the letter **F**. __slur - play the notes legato (smooth)__

i) Identify the cadence at **G** as Perfect, Imperfect or Plagal. __Perfect__

j) Explain the sign at the letter **H**. __Repeat from the beginning__

UltimateMusicTheory.com © Copyright 2013 Gloryland Publishing. All Rights Reserved.

ULTIMATE MUSIC THEORY
INTERMEDIATE EXAM SET #2 - EXAM #2

Total Score: ___ / 100

1. a) Write the following harmonic intervals above each of the given notes. Use whole notes.

    Major 7   diminished 5   Perfect 8   minor 7   Augmented 6

b) Invert the above harmonic intervals in the same clef. Name the inversions.

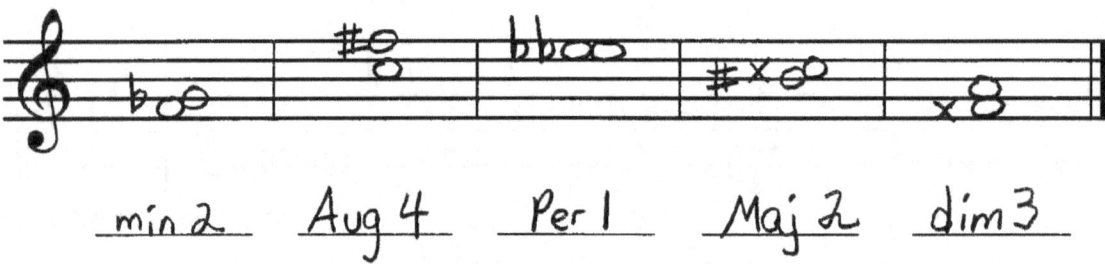

    min 2   Aug 4   Per 1   Maj 2   dim 3

c) Identify the following melodic intervals.

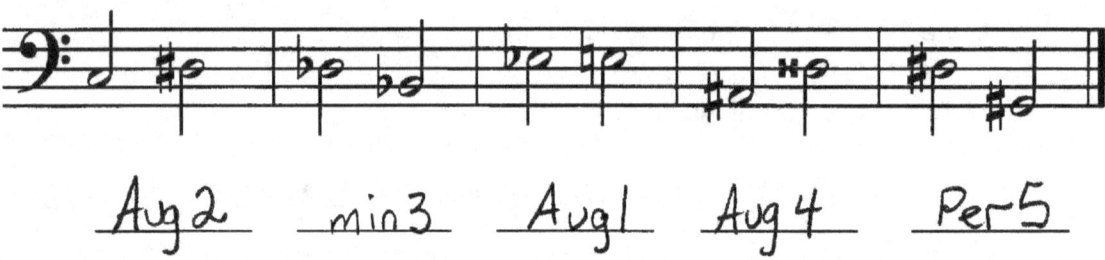

    Aug 2   min 3   Aug 1   Aug 4   Per 5

d) Invert the above melodic intervals in the same clef. Name the inversions.

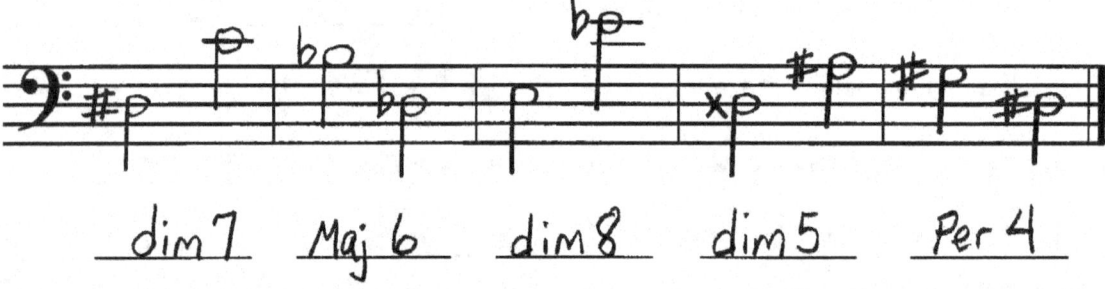

    dim 7   Maj 6   dim 8   dim 5   Per 4

UltimateMusicTheory.com © Copyright 2013 Gloryland Publishing. All Rights Reserved.

ULTIMATE MUSIC THEORY
INTERMEDIATE EXAM SET #2 - EXAM #2

2. a) Write the following Key Signatures in the Bass Clef.

10

The minor key with A as the Supertonic. (g minor)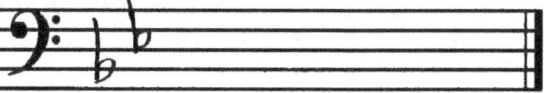

The Major key with D# as the Mediant. (B Major)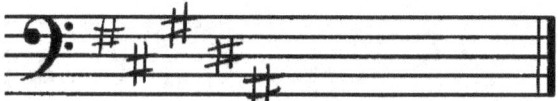

The minor key with C as the Tonic. (c minor)

The Major key with B as the Leading note. (C Major)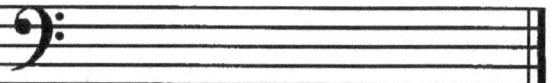

The minor key with F# as the Dominant. (b minor)

b) Name the following notes.

The Supertonic of f sharp minor harmonic.   G#

The Subdominant of e flat minor melodic.   Ab

The Leading note of G flat Major.   F

The Mediant of B flat Major.   D

The Submediant of d minor melodic.   B

ULTIMATE MUSIC THEORY
INTERMEDIATE EXAM SET #2 - EXAM #2

3. The following melody is in the key of E Major.
   a) Transpose the given melody UP a minor third. Use the correct Key Signature. Name the key of the new melody.
   b) Transpose the given melody UP a diminished fifth. Use the correct Key Signature. Name the key of the new melody.

Key: E Major

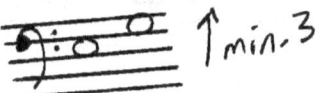

Key: G Major

Key: B♭ Major

UltimateMusicTheory.com © Copyright 2013 Gloryland Publishing. All Rights Reserved.

ULTIMATE MUSIC THEORY
INTERMEDIATE EXAM SET #2 - EXAM #2

4. Write the following scales, ascending and descending, in the given clefs. Use whole notes.

10 a) The enharmonic Tonic Major scale of d sharp minor. Use accidentals. (E♭ Major)

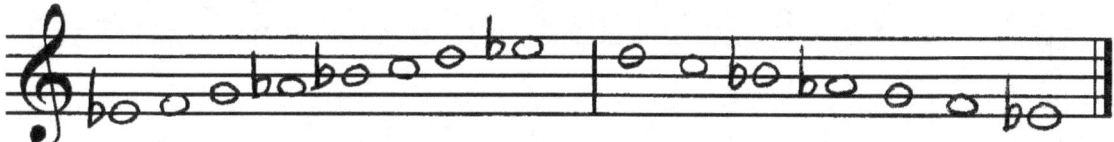

b) The Tonic minor scale, harmonic form, of A flat Major. Use a Key Signature. (a♭ min. harm)

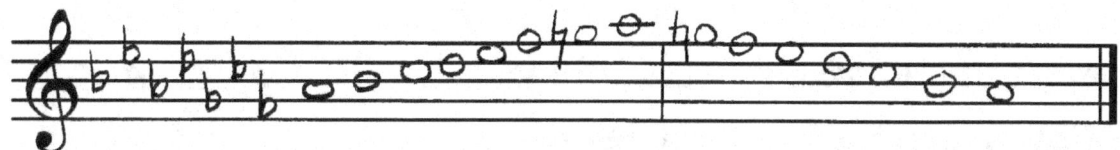

c) The enharmonic relative minor scale, melodic form, of B Major. Use accidentals. (a♭ min. mel.)

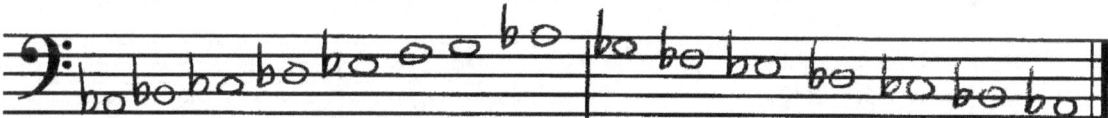

d) Whole Tone scale beginning on G. Use accidentals. Use any standard notation.

e) Chromatic scale beginning on C. Use accidentals. Use any standard notation.

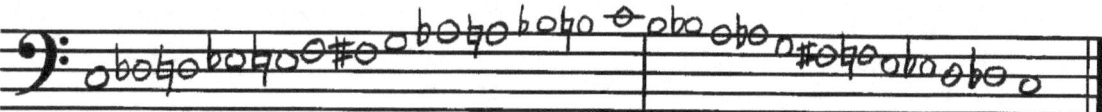

ULTIMATE MUSIC THEORY
INTERMEDIATE EXAM SET #2 - EXAM #2

5. For each of the following cadences, name:
   a) the key.
   b) the type of cadence (Perfect, Plagal or Imperfect).

| Key: | F Major | B Major | b♭ minor |
| Type: | Imperfect | Plagal | Perfect |

c) Write the following triads in solid form in close position. Use whole notes. Use a Key Signature.

The Subdominant triad
of f minor harmonic
in second inversion.

The Supertonic triad
of A Major
in root position.

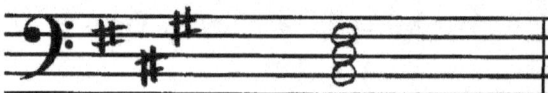

The Dominant triad
of c sharp minor harmonic
in first inversion.

The Tonic triad
of D flat Major
in second inversion.

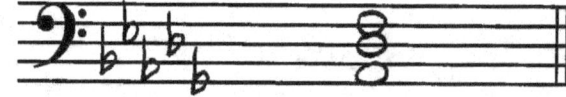

UltimateMusicTheory.com © Copyright 2013 Gloryland Publishing. All Rights Reserved.

ULTIMATE MUSIC THEORY
INTERMEDIATE EXAM SET #2 - EXAM #2

6. For each of the following excerpts:
   a) Name the key.
   b) Add the correct Time Signature below the bracket.

Key: F# Major

Key: D Major

Key: C Minor

c) For each of the following excerpts, add bar lines.

ULTIMATE MUSIC THEORY
INTERMEDIATE EXAM SET #2 - EXAM #2

7. Add rests below each bracket to complete each measure.

10

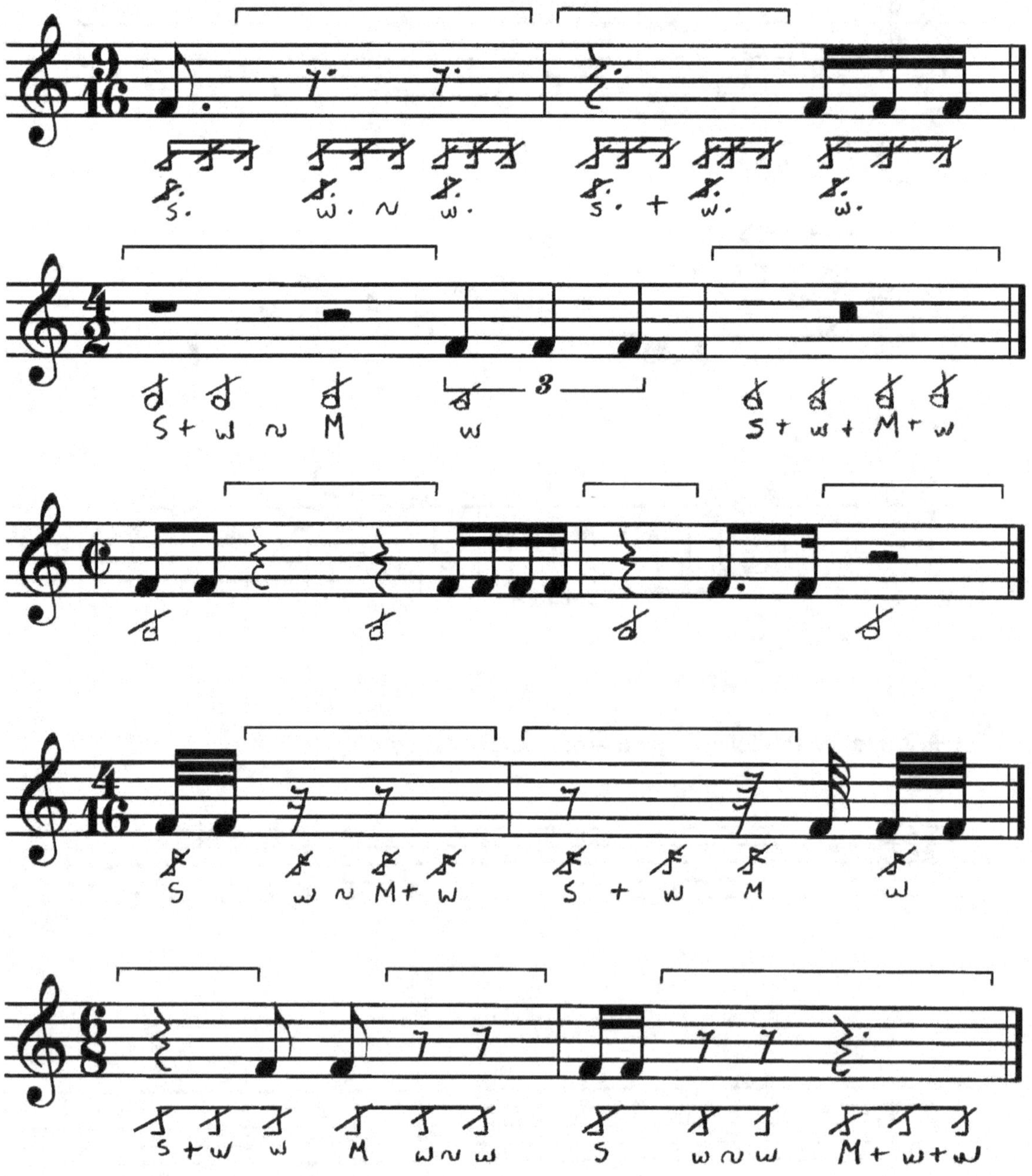

ULTIMATE MUSIC THEORY
INTERMEDIATE EXAM SET #2 - EXAM #2

8. a) Name the following scales as blues, chromatic, Major pentatonic, minor pentatonic, octatonic or whole tone.

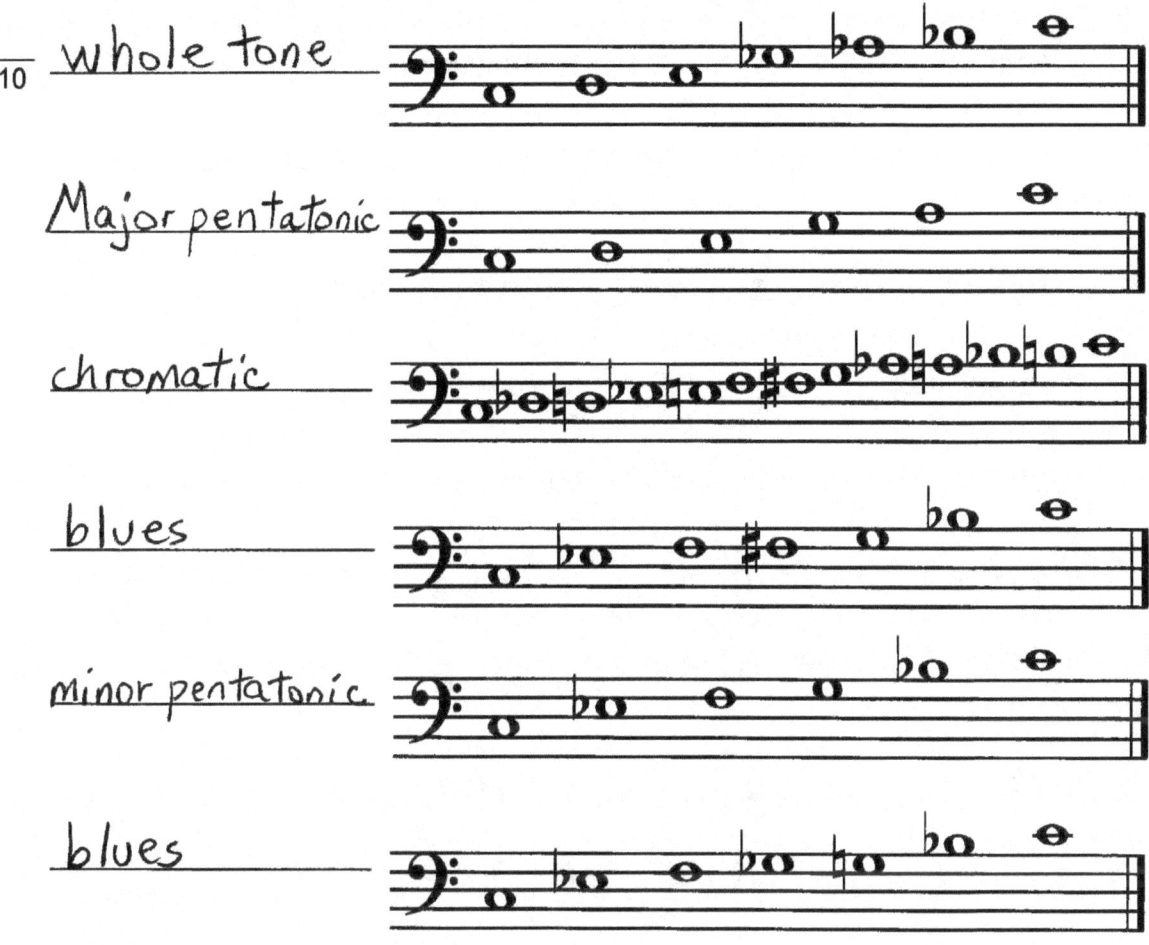

1. whole tone
2. Major pentatonic
3. chromatic
4. blues
5. minor pentatonic
6. blues

b) Identify the root note and the quality/type of each of the following triads.

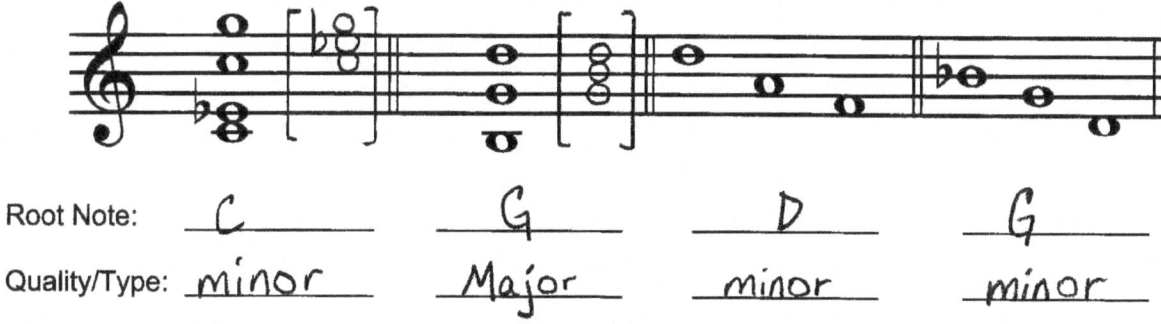

Root Note: C, G, D, G
Quality/Type: minor, Major, minor, minor

ULTIMATE MUSIC THEORY
INTERMEDIATE EXAM SET #2 - EXAM #2

9. Match each musical term with its English definition. (Not all definitions will be used.)

$\frac{}{10}$

Term		Definition
		a) and
spiritoso	e	b) in the manner of
accelerando	i	c) quiet, tranquil
all'	b	d) more
tranquillo	c	e) spirited
vivace	l	f) too much
troppo	f	g) slow and solemn
più	d	h) without
e	a	i) becoming quicker
fortepiano	k	j) brilliant
grave	g	k) loud then suddenly soft
		l) lively, brisk

UltimateMusicTheory.com © Copyright 2013 Gloryland Publishing. All Rights Reserved.

ULTIMATE MUSIC THEORY
INTERMEDIATE EXAM SET #2 - EXAM #2

10. Analyze the following excerpt by answering the questions below.

Tricks, not Treats

Grave

S. McKibbon

a) Name the title of this piece. _Tricks, not Treats_

b) Explain the tempo of this piece. _Grave - slow and solemn_

c) Add the Time Signature directly on the music.

d) Name the notes at the letters: A _D♭_   B _C♯_

e) Name the notes at the letters: C _E_   D _F♭_

f) Name the notes at the letters: E _G♯_   F _A♭_

g) Circle an enharmonic equivalent in this piece. Label it as e.e.

h) Circle a diatonic semitone in this piece. Label it as d.s.

i) Circle a whole tone in this piece. Label it as w.t.

j) How many measures are in this piece? _Three_

UltimateMusicTheory.com © Copyright 2013 Gloryland Publishing. All Rights Reserved.

ULTIMATE MUSIC THEORY
INTERMEDIATE EXAM SET #2 - EXAM #3

Total Score: ___ / 100

1. a) Write the following melodic intervals above each of the given notes. Use half notes.

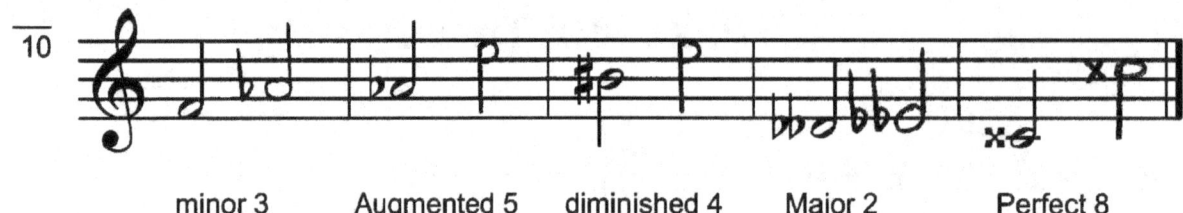

    minor 3   Augmented 5   diminished 4   Major 2   Perfect 8

b) Invert the above melodic intervals in the same clef. Use half notes. Name the inversions.

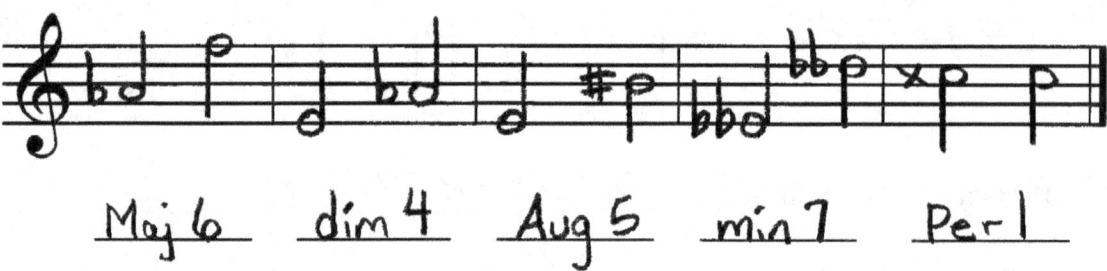

    Maj 6   dim 4   Aug 5   min 7   Per 1

c) Identify the following harmonic intervals.

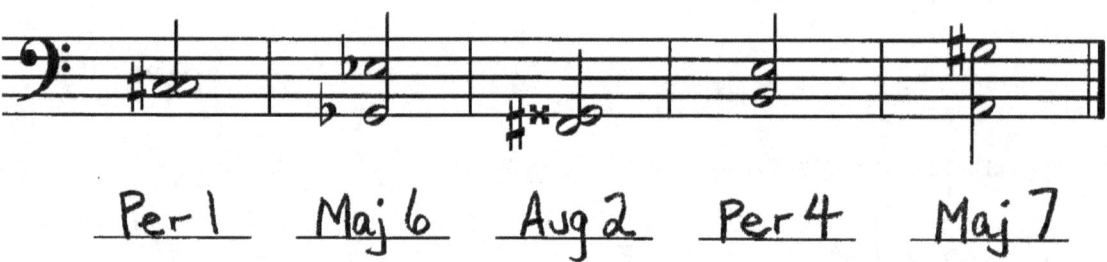

    Per 1   Maj 6   Aug 2   Per 4   Maj 7

d) Invert the above harmonic intervals in the same clef. Use half notes. Name the inversions.

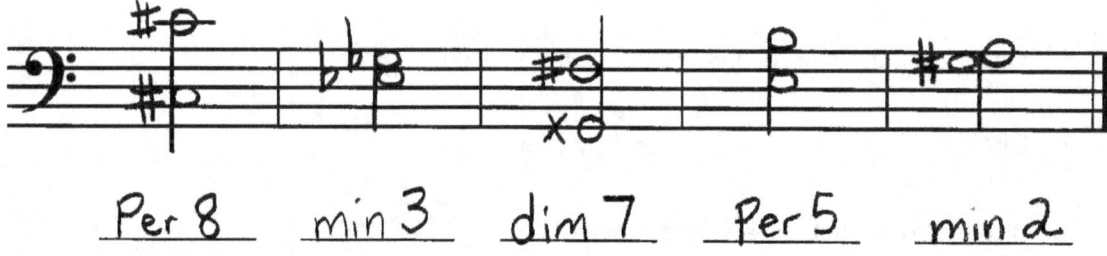

    Per 8   min 3   dim 7   Per 5   min 2

UltimateMusicTheory.com © Copyright 2013 Gloryland Publishing. All Rights Reserved.

ULTIMATE MUSIC THEORY
INTERMEDIATE EXAM SET #2 - EXAM #3

2. a) Write the following triads in the Bass Clef. Use a Key Signature. Use solid form in close position. Use whole notes.

The Subdominant triad of c sharp minor harmonic in first inversion.

The Submediant triad of E flat Major in root position.

The Supertonic triad of D flat Major in second inversion.

The Dominant triad of f minor harmonic in root position.

The Mediant triad of A Major in first inversion.

b) Name the following notes.

The Submediant of C flat Major. — A♭

The Subdominant of f sharp minor harmonic. — B

The Leading note of a minor harmonic. — G#

The Supertonic of B flat Major. — C

The Mediant of d minor harmonic. — F

ULTIMATE MUSIC THEORY
INTERMEDIATE EXAM SET #2 - EXAM #3

3. The following melody is in the key of F Major.
   a) Transpose the given melody UP a minor third. Use the correct Key Signature. Name the key of the new melody.
   b) Transpose the given melody UP an Augmented fourth. Use the correct Key Signature. Name the key of the new melody.

Key: F Major

Key: A♭ Major

Key: B Major

ULTIMATE MUSIC THEORY
INTERMEDIATE EXAM SET #2 - EXAM #3

4. Write the following scales, ascending and descending, in the given clefs. Use whole notes.

10 a) The b flat minor scale, natural form. Use accidentals.

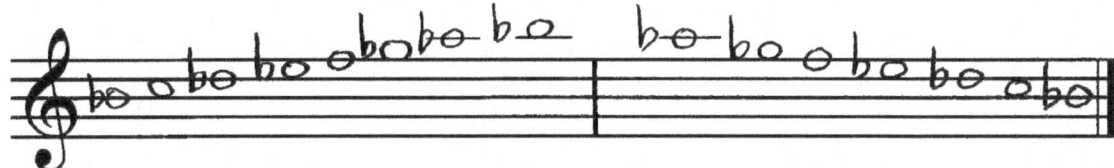

b) The Tonic minor scale, harmonic form, of C Major. Use a Key Signature. (c min. harm.)

c) The relative minor scale, melodic form, of F sharp Major. Use accidentals. (d# min. mel.)

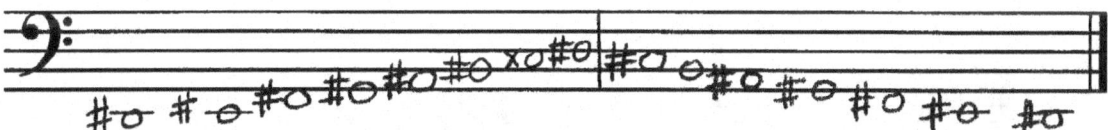

d) Whole Tone scale beginning on B. Use accidentals. Use any standard notation.

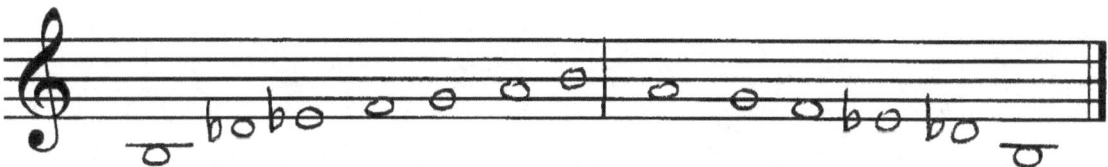

e) Chromatic scale beginning on F. Use accidentals. Use any standard notation.

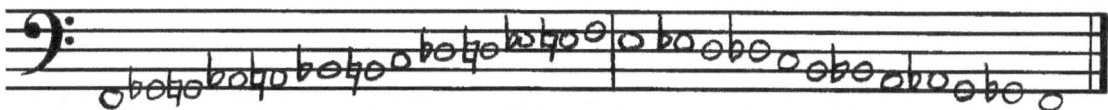

ULTIMATE MUSIC THEORY
INTERMEDIATE EXAM SET #2 - EXAM #3

5. For each of the following cadences, name:
   a) the key.
   b) the type of cadence (Perfect, Plagal or Imperfect).

___
10

Key: B♭ Major   e minor   c♯ minor
Type: Plagal   Imperfect   Perfect

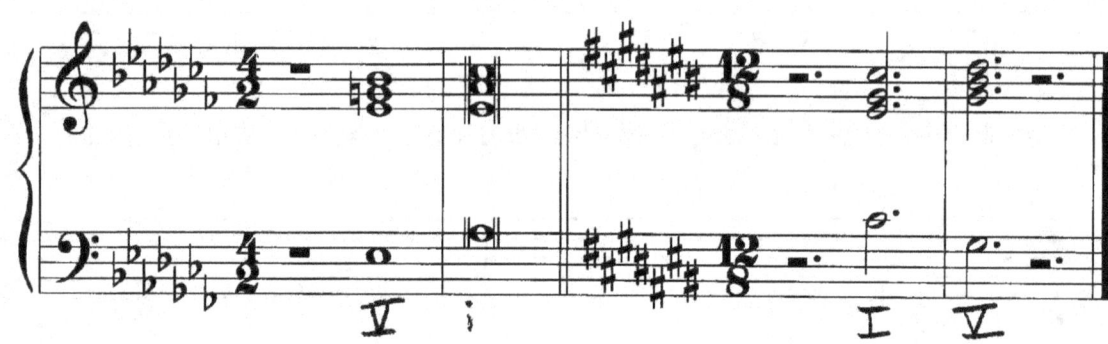

Key: a♭ minor   C♯ Major
Type: Perfect   Imperfect

ULTIMATE MUSIC THEORY
INTERMEDIATE EXAM SET #2 - EXAM #3

6. a) Add the correct Time Signature below the bracket.

b) For each of the following excerpts, add bar lines.

ULTIMATE MUSIC THEORY
INTERMEDIATE EXAM SET #2 - EXAM #3

7. Add rests below each bracket to complete each measure.

ULTIMATE MUSIC THEORY
INTERMEDIATE EXAM SET #2 - EXAM #3

8. a) Name the following scales as blues, chromatic, Major pentatonic, minor pentatonic, octatonic or whole tone.

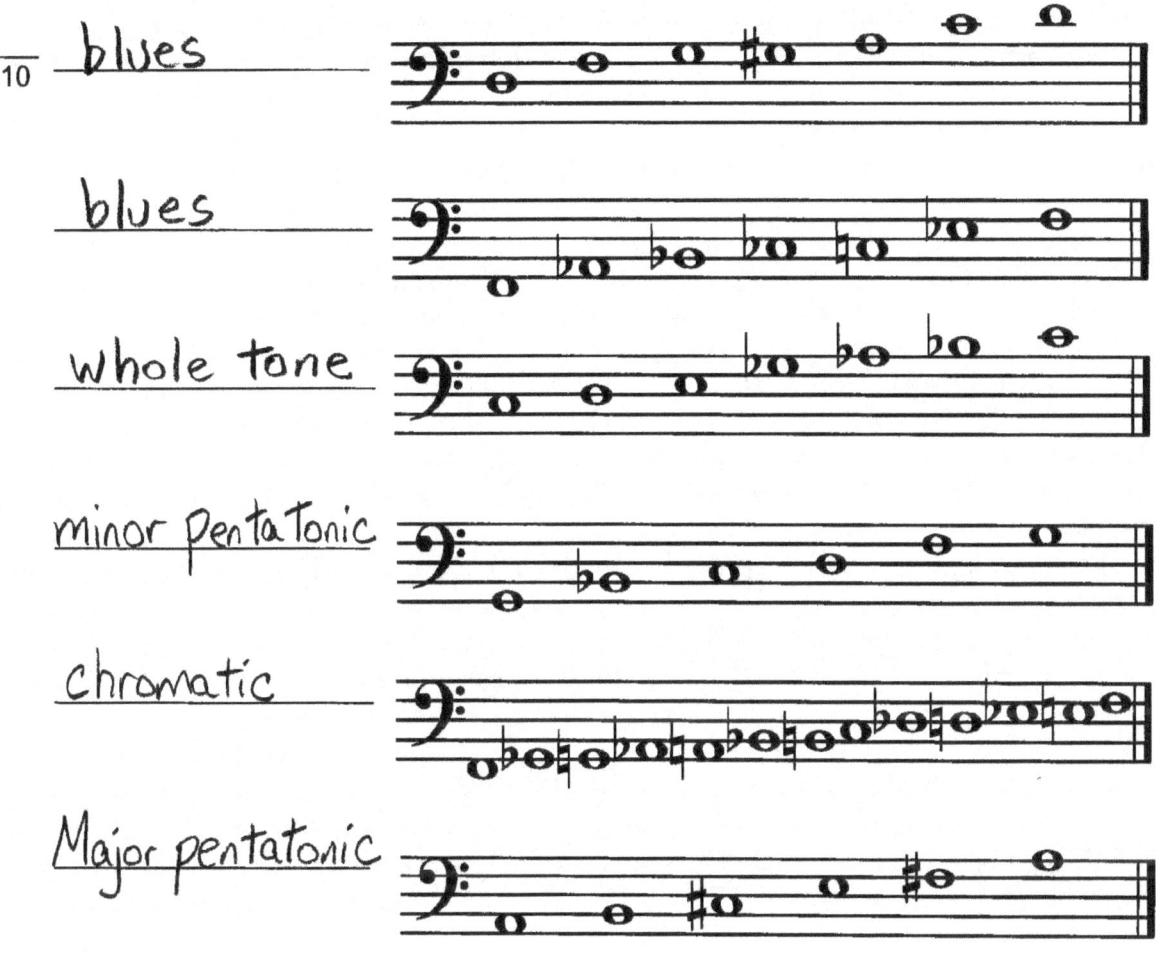

b) Identify the root note and the quality/type of each of the following triads.

Root Note: __E__   __D__   __F__   __E__

Quality/Type: __minor__   __Major__   __Major__   __Major__

ULTIMATE MUSIC THEORY
INTERMEDIATE EXAM SET #2 - EXAM #3

9. Match each musical term with its English definition. (Not all definitions will be used.)

Term — **Definition**

a) one string; depress the left piano pedal

spiritoso — g   b) with movement

meno mosso — i   c) light, nimble, quick

con moto — b   d) sweet, gentle

tre corde — l   e) not as slow as largo

larghetto — e   f) quiet, tranquil

leggiero — c   g) spirited

tranquillo — f   h) as fast as possible

dolce — d   i) less movement, slower

una corda — a   j) fast

presto — k   k) very fast

l) three strings; release the left piano pedal

ULTIMATE MUSIC THEORY
INTERMEDIATE EXAM SET #2 - EXAM #3

10. Analyze the following piece by answering the questions below.

Liam Drops his Spoon

Allegretto S. McKibbon

a) Name the key of this piece. __B♭ Major__

b) Add the Time Signature directly on the music.

c) Name the scale at the letter A. __B♭ Major scale__

d) Name the intervals at the letters: B __Per 4__   C __Per 5__

e) Name the cadence at the letter D. __Imperfect__

f) Explain the sign at the letter E. __forte piano - loud then suddenly soft__

g) Explain the sign at the letter F. __staccato - detached__

h) Name the cadence at the letter G. __Perfect__

i) How many measures are in this piece? __Four__

j) When performed, how many measures are played? __Six__

UltimateMusicTheory.com © Copyright 2013 Gloryland Publishing. All Rights Reserved.

ULTIMATE MUSIC THEORY
INTERMEDIATE EXAM SET #2 - EXAM #4

Total Score: ___ / 100

1. a) Write the following melodic intervals above each of the given notes. Use half notes.

   diminished 5   Perfect 8   Augmented 4   minor 3   minor 7

b) Invert the above melodic intervals in the same clef. Use half notes. Name the inversions.

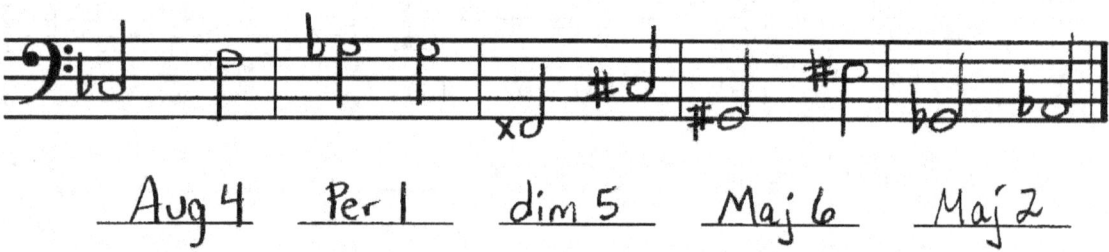

   Aug 4   Per 1   dim 5   Maj 6   Maj 2

c) Identify the following harmonic intervals.

   dim 7   Aug 4   Aug 6   Per 5   Aug 2

d) Invert the above harmonic intervals in the same clef. Use whole notes. Name the inversions.

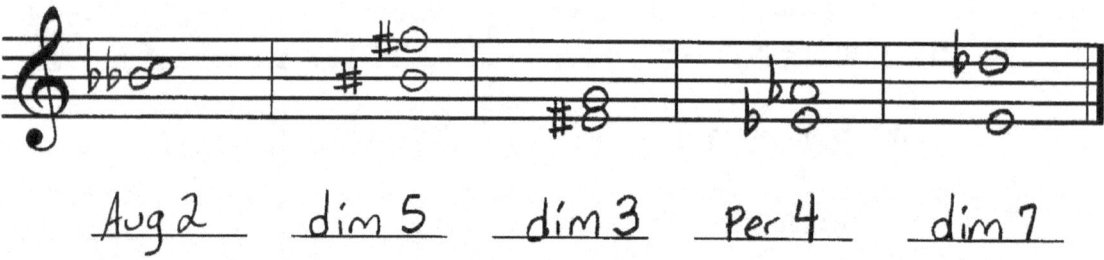

   Aug 2   dim 5   dim 3   Per 4   dim 7

UltimateMusicTheory.com © Copyright 2013 Gloryland Publishing. All Rights Reserved.

ULTIMATE MUSIC THEORY
INTERMEDIATE EXAM SET #2 - EXAM #4

2. a) Write the following triads in the Bass Clef. Use accidentals. Use solid form in close position. Use whole notes.

__10__

The Tonic triad of
c sharp minor harmonic
in first inversion.

The Mediant triad of
E Major
in root position.

The Submediant triad of
D Major
in second inversion.

The Dominant triad of
d minor harmonic
in first inversion.

The Subdominant triad of
B Major
in root position.

b) Name the following notes.

The Leading Note of C flat Major.   B♭

The Submediant of c minor harmonic.   A♭

The Supertonic of a sharp minor harmonic.   B♯

The Subdominant of B flat Major.   E♭

The Mediant of g minor harmonic.   B♭

ULTIMATE MUSIC THEORY
INTERMEDIATE EXAM SET #2 - EXAM #4

3. The following melody is in the key of B flat Major.
   a) Transpose the given melody UP a minor third. Use the correct Key Signature. Name the key of the new melody.
   b) Transpose the given melody UP a Major second. Use the correct Key Signature. Name the key of the new melody.

$\overline{10}$

Key: B flat Major

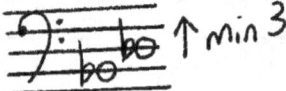

Key: D♭ Major

Key: C Major

ULTIMATE MUSIC THEORY
INTERMEDIATE EXAM SET #2 - EXAM #4

4. Write the following scales, ascending and descending, in the given clefs. Use whole notes.

/10 a) The e flat minor scale, natural form. Use a Key Signature.

b) The Tonic minor scale, melodic form, of B flat Major. Use a Key Signature. (b♭ min. mel.)

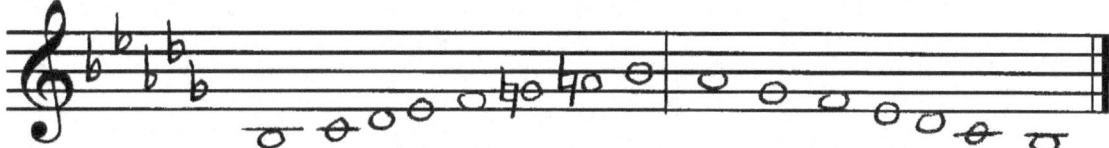

c) The relative minor scale, harmonic form, of B Major. Use accidentals. (g♯ min. harm.)

d) Whole Tone scale beginning on G flat. Use accidentals. Use any standard notation.

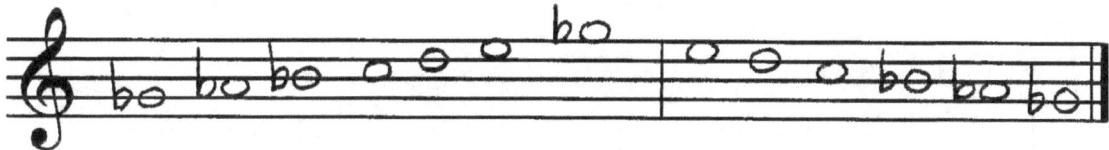

e) Chromatic scale beginning on C sharp. Use accidentals. Use any standard notation.

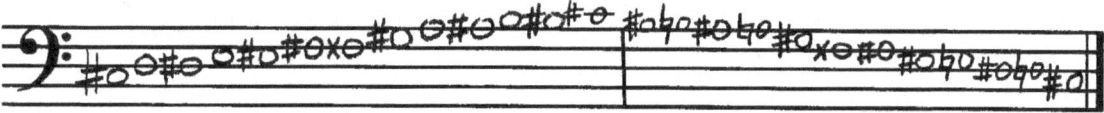

ULTIMATE MUSIC THEORY
INTERMEDIATE EXAM SET #2 - EXAM #4

5. For each of the following cadences, name:
   a) the key.
   b) the type of cadence (Perfect, Plagal or Imperfect).

Key: E♭ Major   b minor   e minor
Type: Plagal   Imperfect   Perfect

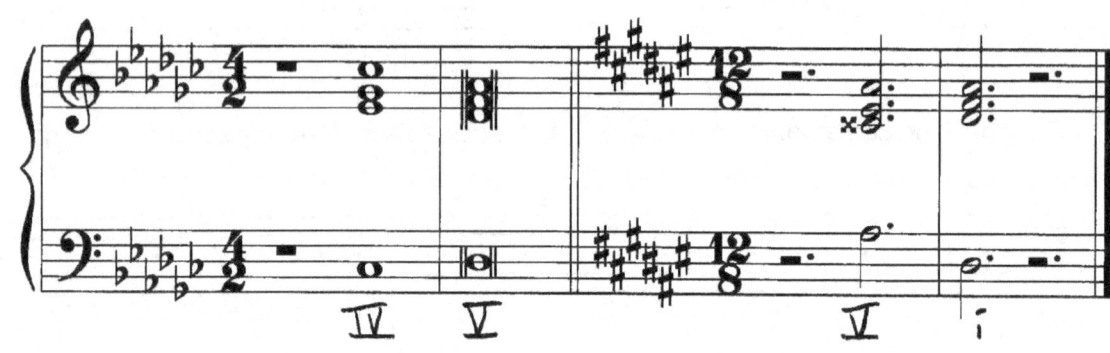

Key: G♭ Major   d♯ minor
Type: Imperfect   Perfect

UltimateMusicTheory.com © Copyright 2013 Gloryland Publishing. All Rights Reserved.

ULTIMATE MUSIC THEORY
INTERMEDIATE EXAM SET #2 - EXAM #4

6. a) Add the correct Time Signature below the bracket.

b) For each of the following excerpts, add bar lines.

ULTIMATE MUSIC THEORY
INTERMEDIATE EXAM SET #2 - EXAM #4

7. Add rests below each bracket to complete each measure.

___
10

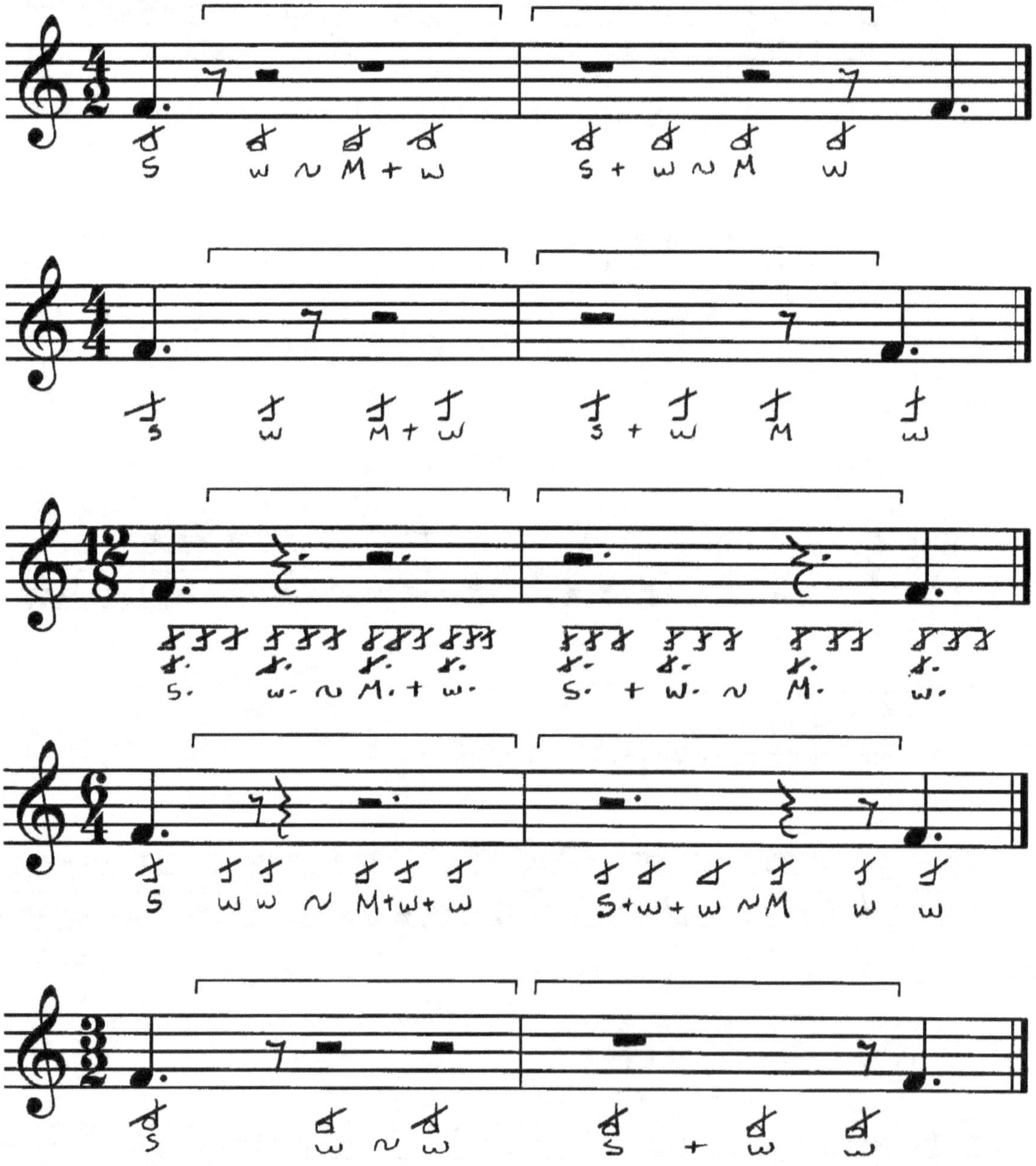

ULTIMATE MUSIC THEORY
INTERMEDIATE EXAM SET #2 - EXAM #4

8. a) Name the following scales as blues, chromatic, Major pentatonic, minor pentatonic, octatonic or whole tone.

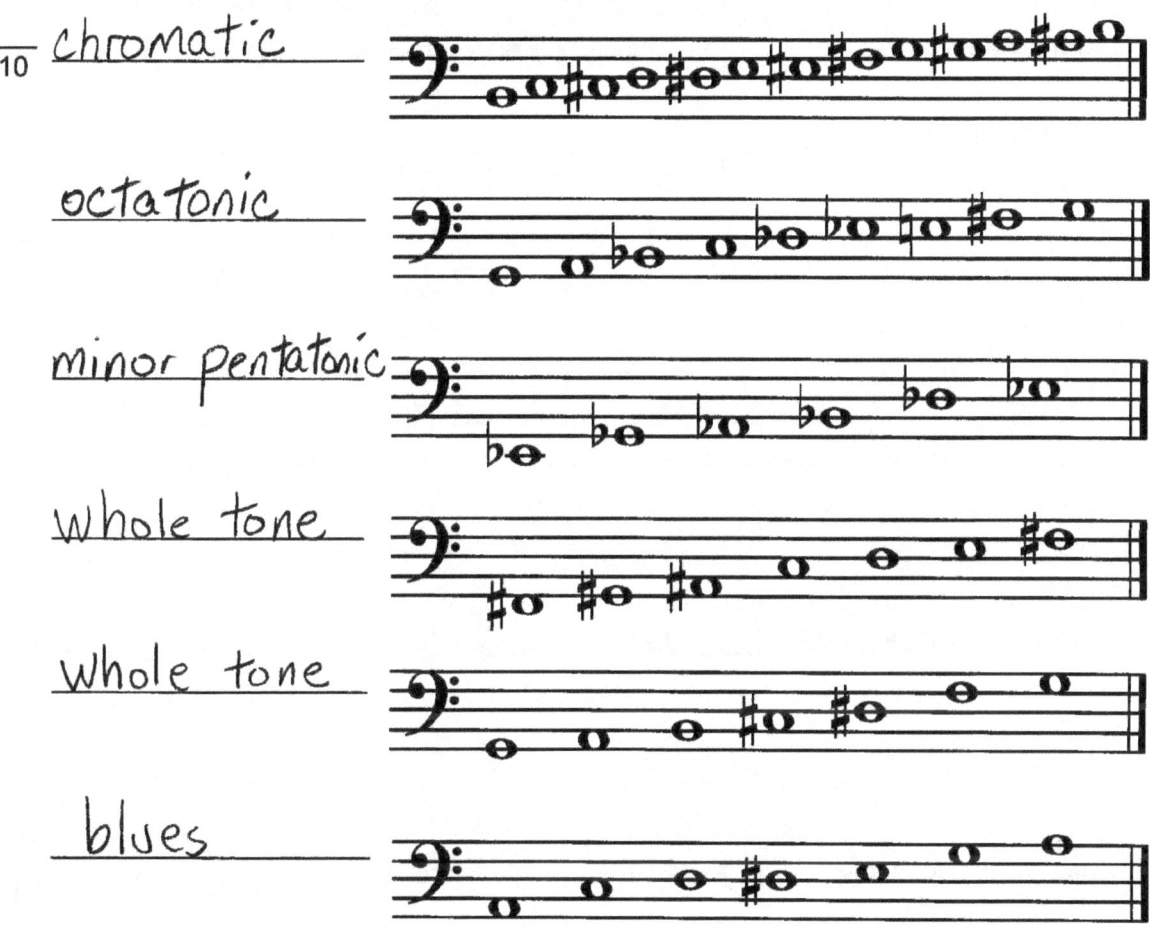

1. chromatic
2. octatonic
3. minor pentatonic
4. whole tone
5. whole tone
6. blues

b) Identify the root note and the quality/type of each of the following triads.

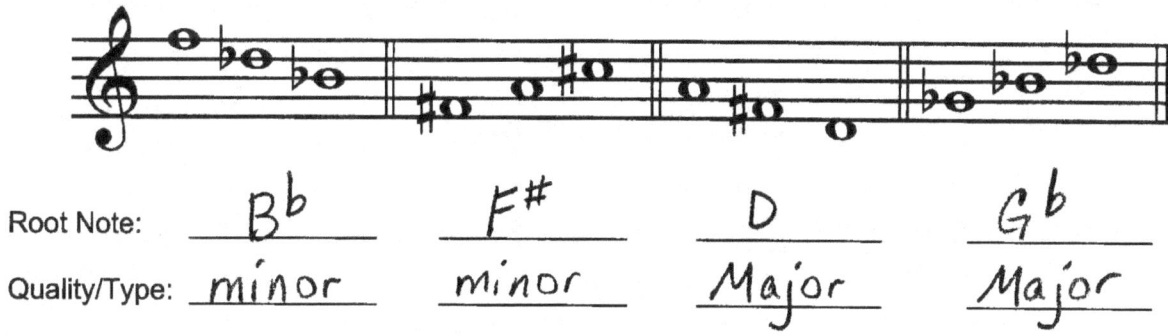

Root Note: Bb, F#, D, Gb
Quality/Type: minor, minor, Major, Major

ULTIMATE MUSIC THEORY
INTERMEDIATE EXAM SET #2 - EXAM #4

9. Choose the Italian term which matches the definition on the left.

Definition		Term Choices	
Example: spirited	[X] spiritoso	[ ] espressivo	[ ] presto
much, very	[ ] ma	[ ] poco	[X] molto
too much	[ ] senza	[X] troppo	[ ] con moto
becoming quicker	[X] accelerando	[ ] crescendo	[ ] diminuendo
loud, then suddenly soft	[ ] fortissimo	[X] fortepiano	[ ] mezzo forte
held, sustained	[X] tenuto	[ ] tie	[ ] staccato
always, continuously	[ ] quasi	[ ] rubato	[X] sempre
quiet, tranquil	[ ] cantabile	[X] tranquillo	[ ] leggiero
sweet, gentle	[X] dolce	[ ] legato	[ ] maestoso
lively, brisk	[ ] presto	[X] vivace	[ ] allegro
Maelzel's metronome	[ ] ed	[X] M.M.	[ ] ma

Total: 10

UltimateMusicTheory.com © Copyright 2013 Gloryland Publishing. All Rights Reserved.

ULTIMATE MUSIC THEORY
INTERMEDIATE EXAM SET #2 - EXAM #4

10. Analyze the following piece of music by answering the questions below.

Owen Can Read!

Animato S. McKibbon

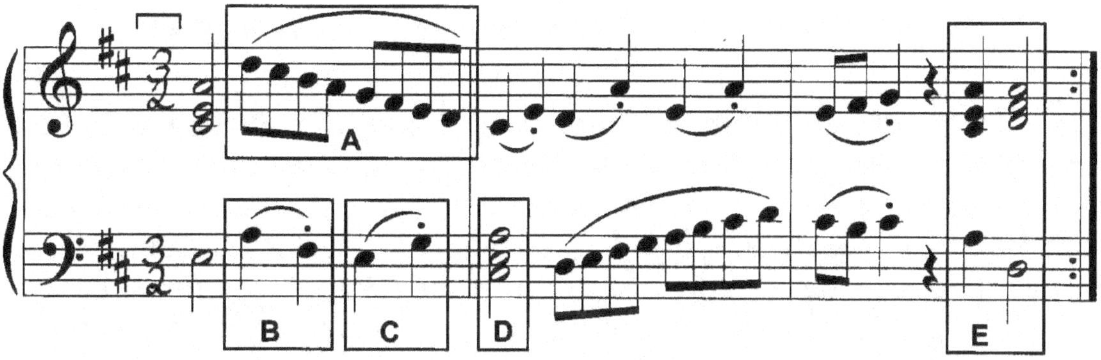

[Musical score with labeled sections A, B, C, D, E]

a) Name the key of this piece. __D Major__

b) Add the Time Signature directly on the music.

c) Name the scale at the letter **A**. __D Major__

d) Name the intervals at the letters: **B** __min 3__   **C** __min 3__

e) At the triad at the letter **D**, name the Root: __A__   Position: __1st inversion__

f) Name the cadence at the letter **E**. __Perfect__

g) How many slurs are in this piece? __Nine__

h) How many staccato notes are in this piece? __Seven__

i) How many measures are in this piece? __Three__

j) When performed, how many measures are played? __Six__

UltimateMusicTheory.com © Copyright 2013 Gloryland Publishing. All Rights Reserved.

Workbooks, Exams, Answers, Online Courses, App & More!

A Proven Step-by-Step System to Learn Theory Faster - from Beginner to Advanced.

Innovative techniques designed to develop a complete understanding of music theory, to enhance sight reading, ear training, creativity, composition and musical expression.

All UMT Series have matching Answer Books!

The UMT Rudiments Series - Beginner A, Beginner B, Beginner C, Prep 1, Prep 2, Basic, Intermediate, Advanced & Complete (All-In-One)

♪ 12 Lessons, Review Tests, and a Final Exam to develop confidence
♪ Music Theory Guide & Chart for fast and easy reference of theory concepts
♪ 80 Flashcards for fun drills to dramatically increase retention & comprehension

Rudiments Exam Series - Preparatory, Basic, Intermediate & Advanced

♪ 8 Exams plus UMT Tips on How to Score 100% on Theory Exams

Each Rudiments Workbook correlates to a Supplemental Workbook.

The UMT Supplemental Series - Prep Level, Level 1, Level 2, Level 3, Level 4, Level 5, Level 6, Level 7, Level 8 & Complete (All-In-One) Level

♪ Form & Analysis and Music History - Composers, Eras & Musical Styles
♪ Melody Writing using ICE - Imagine, Compose & Explore
♪ 12 Lessons, Review Tests, Final Exam and 80 Flashcards for quick study

Supplemental Exam Series - Level 5, Level 6, Level 7 & Level 8

♪ 8 Exams to successfully prepare for nationally recognized Theory Exams

UMT Online Courses, Music Theory App & More

♪ UMT Certification Course, Teachers Membership & Elite Educator Program
♪ Ultimate Music Theory App correlates to the Rudiments Workbooks
♪ Free Resources - Teachers Guide, Music Theory Blogs, videos & downloads

Go To: **UltimateMusicTheory.com**

www.ingramcontent.com/pod-product-compliance
Lightning Source LLC
Chambersburg PA
CBHW081736100526
44591CB00016B/2628